Pesto Pasta Sau

A Culinary Jourr. ⌐ ᵍ
Irresistible Homemade Pesto Sauces

PESTO PASTA SAUCE RECIPES

First edition. November 6, 2023.

Copyright © 2023 Sammy Andrews.

ISBN: 979-8215386149

Written by Sammy Andrews.

Table of Contents

Sammy Andrews

Chapter 1: Introduction to Pesto Magic

Pesto, the magical green sauce that has captured the hearts and taste buds of food lovers around the world, is not just a condiment but a culinary masterpiece. If you've ever marveled at the aroma of freshly crushed basil leaves, the nutty crunch of pine nuts, the sharp bite of garlic, and the salty allure of Parmesan cheese, you're already well on your way to understanding the allure of homemade pesto. In this chapter, we'll embark on a journey to demystify the art of making pesto and explore its endless possibilities.

The Allure of Homemade Pesto

There's something undeniably special about creating your own pesto sauce from scratch. The process itself is a sensory experience that engages your sense of touch, smell, and taste. As you crush fresh basil leaves with mortar and pestle, you release their intoxicating aroma. The grinding of garlic and the toasting of nuts fill the kitchen with anticipation. And when you drizzle in golden olive oil and sprinkle grated Parmesan, you witness the transformation into a vibrant green sauce that beckons you with its freshness.

Pesto: A Flavorful Canvas

Pesto is not just a sauce; it's a canvas for creativity. While the classic Genovese pesto, which hails from the Liguria region of Italy, is undoubtedly a masterpiece in its own right, pesto opens the door to endless variations. This humble sauce is incredibly adaptable, allowing you to experiment with different herbs, nuts, cheeses, and even vegetables. The possibilities are limited only by your imagination.

Pesto's Versatility in the Kitchen

One of the remarkable qualities of pesto is its versatility in the kitchen. It's not just for pasta, although that's its most famous pairing.

Pesto can elevate everything from sandwiches and salads to grilled meats and seafood. Its bold flavors add depth to soups and dressings, and it can even be used as a dip for bread or vegetables.

Beyond Pasta

While we'll certainly delve into the world of pesto-pasta pairings later in this book, we'll also explore creative uses for pesto. Picture a pesto-infused omelet for breakfast, a pesto-stuffed chicken breast for dinner, or a pesto-topped pizza for movie night. Pesto knows no bounds and can effortlessly transform everyday dishes into culinary masterpieces.

Tools and Ingredients for Pesto-Making Success

Before we jump into the exciting world of pesto recipes, let's ensure you have the right tools and ingredients to set yourself up for success. While pesto doesn't require a lot of specialized equipment, a few key items can make the process easier and more enjoyable.

Essential Tools for Pesto-Making

Mortar and Pestle: While you can use a food processor or blender, purists often prefer the traditional method of crushing ingredients with a mortar and pestle. It allows for better control over texture and retains the sauce's vibrant green color.

Cutting Board and Sharp Knife: You'll need these for chopping garlic and other ingredients.

Measuring Spoons and Cups: Precision can be important in pesto recipes, especially when dealing with potent ingredients like garlic and salt.

Micro plane or Grater: This is used for grating hard cheeses like Parmesan or Pecorino.

Quality Olive Oil: Since olive oil is a primary ingredient, it's worth investing in a good-quality extra-virgin olive oil.

Fresh Ingredients: For the best flavor, use fresh herbs, garlic, and other ingredients. Choose organic if possible.

With these tools in your arsenal and a passion for culinary exploration, you're well-equipped to dive into the world of pesto.

In the chapters that follow, we'll explore the classic Genovese pesto, experiment with herb variations, and discover nutty twists that will leave your taste buds tingling with delight. Get ready to embark on a flavorful adventure as we unlock the secrets of homemade pesto and explore its many enchanting variations. The journey begins with the next chapter, where we'll delve into the heart of pesto cuisine: "The Basics of Pesto: Classic Genovese."

Chapter 2: The Basics of Pesto: Classic Genovese

Origin and History of Genovese Pesto

Before we dive into making the perfect Genovese pesto, it's essential to understand its roots and history. Genovese pesto, often referred to simply as "pesto," originated in the picturesque coastal region of Liguria in northwest Italy, particularly in the city of Genoa. This vibrant green sauce, with its signature ingredients, has a storied past that dates back centuries.

The Birthplace of Pesto

Liguria's temperate climate and fertile soil are ideal for cultivating basil, and the region's long history of trading with other Mediterranean cultures introduced it to key ingredients like garlic, olive oil, and Parmesan cheese. These factors converged to give birth to what we now know as pesto.

A Taste of Tradition

The word "pesto" itself comes from the Genoese word "pestâ," which means "to pound" or "to crush." This name perfectly encapsulates the method used to make this sauce: the gentle crushing or grinding of fresh ingredients. Genovese pesto is a celebration of simplicity, highlighting the pure flavors of its primary components: basil, garlic, pine nuts, olive oil, and Parmesan or Pecorino cheese.

Traditional Genovese Pesto Recipe
  Ingredients:

- 2 cups fresh basil leaves, packed
- 2-3 cloves garlic, peeled
- 1/2 cup pine nuts, lightly toasted
- 1/2 cup freshly grated Parmesan cheese

- 1/2 cup extra-virgin olive oil
- Salt, to taste
- Freshly ground black pepper, to taste

Instructions:

Prepare the Basil: Start by washing and drying the basil leaves thoroughly. This ensures that your pesto will have a vibrant green color.

Toast the Pine Nuts: In a dry skillet over medium heat, toast the pine nuts until they become lightly golden and fragrant. Be sure to stir them frequently to prevent burning. Remove from heat and allow them to cool.

Crush the Garlic: Using a mortar and pestle, crush the peeled garlic cloves into a paste. If you don't have a mortar and pestle, you can also finely mince the garlic with a sharp knife.

Combine Ingredients: In the mortar, add the basil leaves, toasted pine nuts, and crushed garlic. Begin gently grinding and crushing the ingredients together, working in a circular motion. This releases the flavors and aromas of the ingredients. Continue until you achieve a coarse paste.

Incorporate the Cheese: Gradually add the grated Parmesan cheese to the mortar and continue to grind and mix. The cheese will help bind the sauce together.

Drizzle in Olive Oil: While still grinding, slowly drizzle in the extra-virgin olive oil until the mixture becomes smooth and cohesive. The olive oil serves to bring all the flavors together and create a creamy consistency.

Season to Taste: Taste the pesto and season with salt and freshly ground black pepper according to your preference. Remember that the Parmesan cheese adds saltiness, so be cautious not to overdo it.

Serve and Enjoy: Your homemade Genovese pesto is ready to be savored! You can immediately toss it with your favorite pasta or store it in an airtight container in the refrigerator for later use. For a delightful pasta dish, cook your pasta of choice and toss it with a few tablespoons of pesto. Garnish with extra grated Parmesan cheese and fresh basil leaves.

Pro Tips:

- Use high-quality, fresh ingredients for the best flavor.
- To prevent basil leaves from turning brown, blanch them briefly in boiling water and then immediately transfer them to an ice water bath before using.
- Experiment with the proportions of ingredients to tailor the pesto to your taste. Some people prefer more garlic or cheese, while others like a bit more olive oil for a creamier texture.

Perfecting the Pesto Texture: Tips and Techniques

Making Genovese pesto is not just about the ingredients; it's also about achieving the perfect texture. Here are some tips and techniques to help you master the art of pesto-making:

Texture Matters

Hand-Crush vs. Blender: While modern kitchen appliances like blenders and food processors can make quick work of pesto, many purists prefer the traditional method of hand-crushing with a mortar and pestle. This method allows for better control over the texture and prevents over-processing, which can result in a duller color and altered flavor.

Balance Ingredients: Achieving the right balance of basil, garlic, nuts, cheese, and oil is crucial. Too much of one ingredient can overpower the others. Start with the classic proportions and adjust to your taste.

Pulse with Care: If you choose to use a food processor or blender, pulse the ingredients in short bursts. Avoid continuous blending, as it can heat the mixture and dull the color.

Gradual Olive Oil Addition: When adding olive oil, do so gradually and in a steady stream. This helps emulsify the sauce and create a smooth, creamy texture.

Storage and Preservation

Air is the Enemy: Pesto can oxidize and turn brown when exposed to air. To prevent this, press plastic wrap directly onto the surface of the pesto or drizzle a thin layer of olive oil on top before sealing it in an airtight container.

Freezing Pesto: If you have leftover pesto or want to make a big batch for later use, consider freezing it. Ice cube trays are an excellent way to portion and freeze small amounts of pesto. Once frozen, transfer the pesto cubes to a zip-top bag for easy storage.

With the fundamentals of Genovese pesto under your belt and the knowledge to perfect its texture, you're well-prepared to explore the world of pesto variations that lie ahead in this cookbook. From herbaceous delights to nutty extravaganzas, we'll continue our journey through the realm of homemade pesto sauces in the upcoming chapters.

Chapter 3: Beyond Basil: Exploring Herb Variations

Beyond Basil: Other Fresh Herbs to Try

While classic Genovese pesto is a beloved favorite, the world of pesto opens up to a kaleidoscope of flavors when you venture beyond basil. Fresh herbs, each with its unique aroma and taste, can breathe new life into your homemade pesto. Let's explore some exciting herb options to elevate your pesto game.

1. Cilantro:

- Flavor Profile: Bright, citrusy, and slightly peppery.
- Pairs Well With: Mexican and Asian-inspired dishes, grilled meats, and seafood.
- Pesto Idea: Cilantro and lime pesto for a zesty twist.

2. Parsley:

- Flavor Profile: Fresh, slightly peppery, and earthy.
- Pairs Well With: Seafood, roasted vegetables, and Mediterranean cuisine.
- Pesto Idea: Flat-leaf parsley pesto for a milder, herbaceous sauce.

3. Mint:

- Flavor Profile: Cool, refreshing, and slightly sweet.
- Pairs Well With: Lamb, peas, and Middle Eastern dishes.
- Pesto Idea: Mint and pea pesto for a vibrant green sauce.

4. Arugula:

- Flavor Profile: Peppery, slightly bitter, and nutty.

- Pairs Well With: Spicy sausage, goat cheese, and salads.
- Pesto Idea: Arugula and walnut pesto for a bold, tangy sauce.

5. Tarragon:

- Flavor Profile: Anise-like, with hints of vanilla and citrus.
- Pairs Well With: Chicken, fish, and creamy sauces.
- Pesto Idea: Tarragon and lemon zest pesto for a unique twist.

6. Dill:

- Flavor Profile: Fresh, tangy, and slightly sweet.
- Pairs Well With: Salmon, cucumber, and yogurt-based dishes.
- Pesto Idea: Dill and cucumber pesto for a refreshing summer sauce.

Herb Combinations for Unique Pesto Flavors
The real magic of herb-infused pesto happens when you combine multiple herbs to create complex and unforgettable flavors. Here are some herb combinations to experiment with:

1. Basil and Mint:

- Flavor Profile: A balance of basil's sweetness and mint's freshness.
- Pairs Well With: Lamb, peas, and Mediterranean-inspired dishes.

2. Parsley and Chives:

- Flavor Profile: Earthy parsley with a hint of onion from chives.
- Pairs Well With: Potatoes, omelets, and roasted vegetables.

3. Cilantro and Jalapeño:

- Flavor Profile: Vibrant cilantro with a spicy kick from jalapeño.
- Pairs Well With: Mexican cuisine, grilled chicken, and tacos.

4. Arugula and Spinach:

- Flavor Profile: Peppery arugula balanced with mild spinach.
- Pairs Well With: Grilled shrimp, pasta salads, and sandwiches.

5. Tarragon and Dill:

- Flavor Profile: Anise-like tarragon with fresh, tangy dill.
- Pairs Well With: Seafood, creamy sauces, and potato dishes.

6. Mint and Basil:

- Flavor Profile: Refreshing mint with basil's sweetness.
- Pairs Well With: Caprese salads, fruit salads, and lamb.

Herb Garden Tips for Homegrown Ingredients

If you're an herb enthusiast, consider growing your own herbs for pesto. A home herb garden can provide you with a constant supply of fresh, aromatic ingredients. Here are some tips to get started:

1. Choose the Right Herbs:

Select herbs that thrive in your climate and soil conditions. Basil, mint, and parsley are excellent choices for beginners.

2. Provide Adequate Sunlight:

Most herbs require at least 6-8 hours of sunlight per day. Ensure your garden receives ample sunlight.

3. Well-Drained Soil:

Use well-draining soil to prevent root rot. You can improve drainage by adding organic matter.

4. Water Wisely:

Herbs generally prefer slightly moist soil. Water them when the top inch of soil feels dry.

5. Pruning and Harvesting:

Regularly prune your herbs to encourage growth and prevent them from becoming leggy. Harvest herbs early in the morning when their oils are most concentrated for the best flavor.

6. Pest Control:

Keep an eye out for pests like aphids and caterpillars. Use natural remedies or pesticides sparingly if needed.

With a little care and attention, your herb garden can yield an abundant harvest of fresh herbs for your homemade pesto creations. The next time you whip up a batch of pesto, you'll know that you've played a part in cultivating its vibrant flavors from seed to sauce.

Chapter 4: Nuts and Bolts: A Guide to Choosing and Toasting Nuts

The Nutty Side of Pesto

Nuts are the unsung heroes of pesto, adding depth, texture, and a delightful nutty flavor to the sauce. While pine nuts are the traditional choice in Genovese pesto, the world of pesto is open to a variety of nuts, each with its unique characteristics. In this chapter, we'll explore the essential role of nuts in pesto, learn how to choose the right nuts, and discover the art of toasting them to enhance their flavor.

Why Nuts Matter

Nuts serve multiple functions in pesto:

- Texture: Nuts add body and creaminess to the sauce, giving it a satisfying mouthfeel.
- Flavor: They contribute their distinct nutty taste, enriching the overall profile of the pesto.
- Thickening Agent: Nuts help bind the ingredients and prevent the sauce from separating.

Selecting the Right Nuts for Your Pesto

Choosing the right nuts for your pesto can significantly impact the sauce's flavor and texture. While pine nuts are the traditional choice, there are various alternatives to explore. Here are some popular options:

1. Pine Nuts:

- Flavor Profile: Mild, buttery, and slightly sweet.
- Pairs Well With: Basil-based pesto, Mediterranean dishes, and salads.

Notes: Pine nuts are the classic choice for Genovese pesto, known for their creamy texture and subtle flavor.

2. Walnuts:

- Flavor Profile: Earthy, slightly bitter, and rich.
- Pairs Well With: Arugula, spinach, and herb-heavy pestos.

Notes: Walnuts are a versatile option and can add a pleasant bitterness to your pesto.

3. Almonds:

- Flavor Profile: Nutty, slightly sweet, and crunchy.
- Pairs Well With: Cilantro, parsley, and citrus-infused pestos.

Notes: Almonds offer a delightful crunch and a mild nutty flavor.

4. Pecans:

- Flavor Profile: Sweet, buttery, and rich.
- Pairs Well With: Sage, sage, and pecorino cheese.

Notes: Pecans lend a sweet, caramelized note to your pesto.

5. Cashews:

- Flavor Profile: Creamy, mild, and slightly sweet.
- Pairs Well With: Thai-inspired pestos and coconut-based sauces.

Notes: Cashews create a velvety texture and a subtle, sweet undertone.

When selecting nuts, consider the flavor profile of the pesto you want to create and experiment with different nuts to find your favorite combination. Keep in mind that you can also mix nuts for a unique flavor profile.

Toasting Nuts to Enhance Flavor

Toasting nuts is a simple yet effective technique that can elevate the flavor of your pesto. It intensifies their nuttiness, adds a delightful aroma, and enhances the overall depth of your sauce. Here's how to toast nuts:

Ingredients:

- Nuts of your choice (e.g., pine nuts, walnuts, almonds, etc.)

Instructions:

Prepare a Dry Skillet: Heat a dry, non-stick skillet or frying pan over medium-low heat. There's no need to add any oil.

Add the Nuts: Place the nuts in a single layer in the heated skillet. Spread them out evenly for even toasting.

Keep an Eye on Them: Toast the nuts for 3-5 minutes, stirring frequently. Pay close attention to avoid burning; nuts can go from golden to burnt quickly.

Watch for Color and Aroma: The nuts are ready when they turn a light golden brown and release a fragrant, toasty aroma.

Cool Completely: Transfer the toasted nuts to a plate or a baking sheet to cool. They will continue to cook slightly if left in the hot skillet, so it's essential to remove them promptly.

Use as Directed: Once cooled, use the toasted nuts in your pesto recipe as directed. They'll bring a robust, nutty flavor to your sauce.

Pro Tips:

- Always toast nuts over low to medium-low heat to prevent burning.
- Use a dry skillet without added oil to ensure even toasting.
- Don't overcrowd the pan; a single layer of nuts allows for more even toasting.

Toasted nuts can take your homemade pesto to the next level, providing a delightful contrast to the fresh herbs and adding depth to the overall flavor profile. Feel free to experiment with different nut varieties and toasting times to find your preferred level of nuttiness.

Chapter 5: Cheese Please: The Role of Cheese in Pesto

The Cheesy Component in Pesto

Cheese is an essential ingredient in many pesto recipes, contributing creaminess, umami, and a salty kick to the sauce. It plays a crucial role in balancing the flavors and binding the other ingredients together. In this chapter, we'll delve into the world of cheese in pesto, explore the differences between Parmesan and Pecorino, and consider non-dairy cheese alternatives for those with dietary preferences or restrictions.

The Cheese's Role

Cheese in pesto serves several key functions:

- Flavor Enhancement: It adds a salty and savory dimension to the sauce, enhancing the overall taste.

- Texture and Creaminess: Cheese contributes to the creamy texture of pesto, making it a luscious sauce that clings to pasta.

- Binding Agent: Cheese helps bind the ingredients together, preventing separation.

Parmesan vs. Pecorino: Cheese Selection Tips

Two classic cheeses often used in pesto are Parmesan and Pecorino. While they share some similarities, each brings its unique character to the sauce. Let's explore their differences and how to choose the right one for your pesto:

Parmesan Cheese

- Flavor Profile: Salty, nutty, and slightly sweet.
- Texture: Hard and granular when grated.

- Pairs Well With: Basil-based pesto, milder herb pestos, and dishes with a delicate balance of flavors.

Notes: Parmesan is the more commonly used cheese in traditional Genovese pesto. Its subtle sweetness complements the fresh basil and other ingredients.

Pecorino Cheese

- Flavor Profile: Salty, tangy, and more robust.
- Texture: Hard and crumbly when grated.
- Pairs Well With: Pesto featuring strong herbs like arugula or dishes that benefit from a sharper cheese flavor.

Notes: Pecorino brings a distinctive tanginess to pesto and pairs exceptionally well with peppery herbs and ingredients.

Choosing Between Parmesan and Pecorino: The choice between Parmesan and Pecorino ultimately depends on your flavor preference and the ingredients you plan to pair with your pesto. You can also experiment by blending the two for a unique flavor profile that balances sweetness and tang.

Exploring Non-Dairy Cheese Alternatives

For those who follow a vegan or dairy-free diet or have lactose intolerance, there are excellent non-dairy cheese alternatives that can replicate the creamy, cheesy goodness of traditional pesto. Here are some options to consider:

1. Nutritional Yeast:

- Flavor Profile: Nutty, savory, and slightly cheesy.
- Texture: Flakes or powder.
- Pairs Well With: Vegan pesto, dairy-free pasta dishes, and plant-based sauces.

Notes: Nutritional yeast is a popular choice for adding a cheesy flavor to vegan or dairy-free pesto. It's a source of vitamin B12 and often used in plant-based cooking.

2. Vegan Parmesan:

- Flavor Profile: Similar to Parmesan but without dairy.
- Texture: Grated or powdered.
- Pairs Well With: Vegan pesto, dairy-free pasta dishes, and salads.

Notes: Vegan Parmesan is made from nuts, seeds, or nutritional yeast and mimics the salty, savory flavor of traditional Parmesan.

3. Cashew Cream:

- Flavor Profile: Creamy and mildly nutty.
- Texture: Creamy, like dairy-based cream.
- Pairs Well With: Vegan creamy pesto sauces and dishes.

Notes: Cashew cream can provide the creamy richness typically associated with cheese in pesto. It's a versatile dairy substitute.

4. Tofu:

- Flavor Profile: Mild, neutral, and creamy.
- Texture: Silken or firm tofu can be blended for a creamy texture.
- Pairs Well With: Vegan pesto variations and sauces.

Notes: Silken tofu, when blended, can provide creaminess to vegan pesto sauces without adding a strong flavor.

Experimenting with non-dairy cheese alternatives can lead to exciting discoveries in the world of dairy-free pesto. These options allow you to enjoy the flavors and textures of pesto while accommodating dietary preferences and restrictions.

Chapter 6: Pesto Without Boundaries: Nut-Free Variations

Nut Allergies and Nut-Free Pesto Options

Pesto is a beloved sauce for many, but it can pose challenges for those with nut allergies. Nut allergies are among the most common food allergies, and for those affected, enjoying classic pesto recipes can be risky. However, the world of pesto offers a wide range of nut-free alternatives that are equally delicious and safe to enjoy. In this chapter, we'll explore the reasons behind nut allergies, discover nut-free alternatives, and dive into nut-free pesto recipes that everyone can savor.

Understanding Nut Allergies

Nut allergies are allergic reactions to proteins found in tree nuts and peanuts. These allergies can range from mild to severe, with symptoms that may include itching, hives, swelling, abdominal pain, and even life-threatening anaphylaxis.

Seeds and Other Nut Alternatives

When creating nut-free pesto, it's essential to find suitable alternatives that provide texture, flavor, and creaminess. Seeds and other ingredients can fill the nut void. Here are some nut-free alternatives to consider:

1. Sunflower Seeds:

- Flavor Profile: Mild, nutty, and slightly sweet.
- Texture: Crunchy when toasted; creamy when blended.
- Pairs Well With: Basil, spinach, and other herbs in pesto.

Notes: Sunflower seeds are a popular choice for nut-free pesto. Toasting them enhances their nuttiness, and they blend well to create a creamy sauce.

2. Pumpkin Seeds (Pepitas):

- Flavor Profile: Nutty, earthy, and slightly sweet.
- Texture: Crunchy when toasted; creamy when blended.
- Pairs Well With: Cilantro, parsley, and Mexican-inspired pestos.

Notes: Pumpkin seeds add a unique flavor and a satisfying crunch to nut-free pesto recipes.

3. Hemp Seeds:

- Flavor Profile: Mild, slightly nutty, and earthy.
- Texture: Creamy when blended.
- Pairs Well With: Spinach, arugula, and herb-heavy pestos.

Notes: Hemp seeds are rich in omega-3 fatty acids and protein, making them a nutritious addition to pesto.

4. Sesame Seeds (Tahini):

- Flavor Profile: Nutty, rich, and slightly bitter.
- Texture: Creamy when blended.
- Pairs Well With: Mediterranean-inspired pestos and dishes.

Notes: Sesame seeds, when ground into tahini, can create a velvety, nut-free pesto with a distinct flavor.

Nut-Free Pesto Recipes

Let's explore some delicious nut-free pesto recipes that will allow everyone to enjoy this flavorful sauce without concern for nut allergies.

Recipe 1: Nut-Free Sunflower Seed Pesto
Ingredients:

- 2 cups fresh basil leaves, packed
- 1/3 cup sunflower seeds, toasted
- 2-3 cloves garlic, peeled

- 1/2 cup grated Parmesan or vegan Parmesan
- 1/2 cup extra-virgin olive oil
- Salt and freshly ground black pepper, to taste

Instructions:

Prepare the Basil: Wash and dry the basil leaves thoroughly.

Toast the Sunflower Seeds: In a dry skillet over medium-low heat, toast the sunflower seeds until lightly golden and fragrant. Stir frequently to prevent burning. Allow them to cool.

Crush the Garlic: Use a mortar and pestle to crush the peeled garlic cloves into a paste.

Combine Ingredients: In the mortar, add the basil leaves, toasted sunflower seeds, and crushed garlic. Begin gently grinding and crushing the ingredients together until you achieve a coarse paste.

Incorporate the Cheese: Gradually add the grated Parmesan cheese to the mortar and continue to grind and mix.

Drizzle in Olive Oil: While still grinding, slowly drizzle in the extra-virgin olive oil until the mixture becomes smooth and cohesive.

Season to Taste: Taste the pesto and season with salt and freshly ground black pepper according to your preference. Remember that the Parmesan cheese adds saltiness, so be cautious not to overdo it.

Serve and Enjoy: Your nut-free sunflower seed pesto is ready to be enjoyed! Toss it with your favorite pasta or use it as a sauce for other dishes.

Recipe 2: Nut-Free Pumpkin Seed Pesto

Ingredients:

- 2 cups fresh cilantro leaves, packed
- 1/3 cup pumpkin seeds (pepitas), toasted
- 2 cloves garlic, peeled
- 1/2 cup grated Pecorino or vegan Pecorino

- 1/2 cup extra-virgin olive oil
- Salt and freshly ground black pepper, to taste

Instructions:
Prepare the Cilantro: Wash and dry the cilantro leaves thoroughly.

Toast the Pumpkin Seeds: In a dry skillet over medium-low heat, toast the pumpkin seeds until lightly golden and fragrant. Stir frequently to prevent burning. Allow them to cool.

Crush the Garlic: Use a mortar and pestle to crush the peeled garlic cloves into a paste.

Combine Ingredients: In the mortar, add the cilantro leaves, toasted pumpkin seeds, and crushed garlic. Begin gently grinding and crushing the ingredients together until you achieve a coarse paste.

Incorporate the Cheese: Gradually add the grated Pecorino cheese to the mortar and continue to grind and mix.

Drizzle in Olive Oil: While still grinding, slowly drizzle in the extra-virgin olive oil until the mixture becomes smooth and cohesive.

Season to Taste: Taste the pesto and season with salt and freshly ground black pepper according to your preference. Remember that the Pecorino cheese adds saltiness, so be cautious not to overdo it.

Serve and Enjoy: Your nut-free pumpkin seed pesto is ready to be enjoyed! It pairs wonderfully with pasta, roasted vegetables, or grilled meats.

These nut-free pesto recipes provide delicious alternatives for those with nut allergies, ensuring that everyone can savor the wonderful flavors of pesto without worry. Feel free to customize these recipes with your favorite herbs and ingredients for a personalized twist.

Chapter 7: Roasted and Toasted: Unique Nutty Twists

Elevating Pesto with Roasted Nuts

Toasting nuts is one way to enhance their flavor, but taking it a step further with roasting can elevate your pesto to new heights. Roasting nuts intensifies their nuttiness, adds depth, and imparts a delightful aroma to your sauce. In this chapter, we'll explore the art of roasting nuts for pesto, experiment with creative nut combinations, and unveil recipes that showcase the rich flavors of roasted nut pesto.

The Magic of Roasted Nuts

Roasting nuts is a simple yet transformative technique that unlocks their full potential. The process involves exposing the nuts to dry heat, intensifying their flavors through Maillard browning and caramelization. Roasted nuts are bolder, richer, and even more aromatic than their untoasted counterparts.

Creative Nut Combinations

While classic pesto recipes often rely on single nut varieties, there's a world of flavor to discover by combining different nuts. Mixing nuts can result in complex, nuanced pesto sauces that surprise and delight your taste buds. Here are some creative nut combinations to explore:

1. Almond and Cashew:

- Flavor Profile: Creamy, sweet, and slightly nutty.
- Pairs Well With: Basil, spinach, and herb-heavy pestos.

Notes: This combination offers a creamy texture with a balance of sweetness and nuttiness.

2. Walnut and Pecan:

- Flavor Profile: Rich, earthy, and slightly bitter.
- Pairs Well With: Arugula, sage, and hearty herb pestos.

Notes: The combination of walnuts and pecans creates a robust, rustic pesto.

3. Pine Nut and Pistachio:

- Flavor Profile: Buttery, slightly sweet, and vibrant.
- Pairs Well With: Traditional Genovese pesto and fresh herb pestos.

Notes: Pine nuts and pistachios offer a luxurious, rich pesto experience.

4. Hazelnut and Macadamia:

- Flavor Profile: Creamy, buttery, and mildly sweet.
- Pairs Well With: Mint, parsley, and lemon-infused pestos.

Notes: Hazelnuts and macadamia nuts create a velvety, indulgent pesto.

5. Brazil Nut and Pumpkin Seed:

- Flavor Profile: Earthy, nutty, and slightly sweet.
- Pairs Well With: Cilantro, parsley, and Latin-inspired pestos.

Notes: This combination adds a South American twist to your pesto.

Recipes for Roasted Nut Pesto
Let's explore two delightful recipes that feature the rich and nuanced flavors of roasted nut pesto.

Recipe 1: Roasted Almond and Cashew Pesto
Ingredients:

- 2 cups fresh basil leaves, packed
- 1/3 cup roasted almonds
- 1/3 cup roasted cashews
- 2-3 cloves garlic, peeled
- 1/2 cup grated Parmesan or vegan Parmesan
- 1/2 cup extra-virgin olive oil
- Salt and freshly ground black pepper, to taste

Instructions:
Prepare the Basil: Wash and dry the basil leaves thoroughly.

Roast the Nuts: Preheat your oven to 350°F (175°C). Spread the almonds and cashews on a baking sheet and roast for about 8-10 minutes or until they are fragrant and lightly browned. Remove from the oven and let them cool.

Crush the Garlic: Use a mortar and pestle to crush the peeled garlic cloves into a paste.

Combine Ingredients: In the mortar, add the basil leaves, roasted almonds, roasted cashews, and crushed garlic. Begin gently grinding and crushing the ingredients together until you achieve a coarse paste.

Incorporate the Cheese: Gradually add the grated Parmesan cheese to the mortar and continue to grind and mix.

Drizzle in Olive Oil: While still grinding, slowly drizzle in the extra-virgin olive oil until the mixture becomes smooth and cohesive.

Season to Taste: Taste the pesto and season with salt and freshly ground black pepper according to your preference. Remember that the Parmesan cheese adds saltiness, so be cautious not to overdo it.

Serve and Enjoy: Your roasted almond and cashew pesto is ready to be savored! Pair it with your favorite pasta or use it as a sauce for other dishes.

Recipe 2: Roasted Walnut and Pecan Pesto
Ingredients:

- 2 cups fresh arugula leaves, packed
- 1/3 cup roasted walnuts
- 1/3 cup roasted pecans
- 2-3 cloves garlic, peeled
- 1/2 cup grated Pecorino or vegan Pecorino
- 1/2 cup extra-virgin olive oil
- Salt and freshly ground black pepper, to taste

Instructions:
Prepare the Arugula: Wash and dry the arugula leaves thoroughly.

Roast the Nuts: Preheat your oven to 350°F (175°C). Spread the walnuts and pecans on a baking sheet and roast for about 8-10 minutes or until they are fragrant and lightly browned. Remove from the oven and let them cool.

Crush the Garlic: Use a mortar and pestle to crush the peeled garlic cloves into a paste.

Combine Ingredients: In the mortar, add the arugula leaves, roasted walnuts, roasted pecans, and crushed garlic. Begin gently grinding and crushing the ingredients together until you achieve a coarse paste.

Incorporate the Cheese: Gradually add the grated Pecorino cheese to the mortar and continue to grind and mix.

Drizzle in Olive Oil: While still grinding, slowly drizzle in the extra-virgin olive oil until the mixture becomes smooth and cohesive.

Season to Taste: Taste the pesto and season with salt and freshly ground black pepper according to your preference. Remember that the Pecorino cheese adds saltiness, so be cautious not to overdo it.

Serve and Enjoy: Your roasted walnut and pecan pesto is ready to be enjoyed! It pairs wonderfully with pasta, roasted vegetables, or grilled meats.

Roasted nut pesto adds a layer of complexity and depth to your pesto creations, making them perfect for special occasions or when you want to impress your guests. Don't hesitate to experiment with different nut combinations to discover your favorite roasted nut pesto flavor profile.

Chapter 8: Green Goodness: Incorporating Leafy Greens

Adding Vibrancy with Leafy Greens

While basil is the star of classic pesto, there's a world of leafy greens waiting to elevate your pesto game. Incorporating a variety of greens not only adds vibrant color but also introduces unique flavors and nutrients to your sauce. In this chapter, we'll explore the art of incorporating leafy greens into pesto, mix different greens for balanced flavor, and create wholesome green pesto recipes that celebrate the beauty of greens.

The Power of Leafy Greens

Leafy greens are nutritional powerhouses, packed with vitamins, minerals, and antioxidants. They bring freshness, vibrancy, and a delightful green hue to your pesto. By experimenting with different greens, you can create pesto sauces that are as nutritious as they are delicious.

Mixing Greens for Balanced Flavor

Creating pesto with a variety of leafy greens allows you to balance flavors and textures. Each green has its unique profile, from peppery arugula to earthy spinach and the mild sweetness of kale. Here are some green combinations to consider:

1. Basil and Spinach:

- Flavor Profile: Aromatic, slightly sweet, and mild.
- Pairs Well With: Traditional Genovese pesto, pasta salads, and sandwiches.

Notes: This combination maintains the classic pesto flavor while adding a boost of nutrients from spinach.

2. Arugula and Kale:

- Flavor Profile: Peppery, earthy, and mildly sweet.

- Pairs Well With: Hearty dishes, such as whole-grain pasta or roasted vegetables.

Notes: Arugula's boldness complements the earthiness of kale for a robust pesto.

3. Cilantro and Parsley:

- Flavor Profile: Bright, citrusy, and slightly peppery.
- Pairs Well With: Mexican-inspired dishes, grilled chicken, and seafood.

Notes: This combination adds a zesty twist to your pesto, perfect for Southwestern flavors.

4. Baby Spinach and Mint:

- Flavor Profile: Mild, refreshing, and slightly sweet.
- Pairs Well With: Mediterranean-inspired dishes, lamb, and fresh salads.

Notes: The addition of mint provides a cooling, aromatic element to the pesto.

5. Swiss Chard and Watercress:

- Flavor Profile: Earthy, slightly bitter, and peppery.
- Pairs Well With: Creamy pasta dishes and dishes that benefit from a touch of bitterness.

Notes: This combination adds complexity with its unique flavors.

Wholesome Green Pesto Recipes

Let's explore two wholesome green pesto recipes that embrace the goodness of leafy greens.

Recipe 1: Spinach and Basil Pesto
Ingredients:

- 2 cups fresh basil leaves, packed
- 2 cups fresh baby spinach, packed
- 1/3 cup pine nuts, toasted
- 2-3 cloves garlic, peeled
- 1/2 cup grated Parmesan or vegan Parmesan
- 1/2 cup extra-virgin olive oil
- Salt and freshly ground black pepper, to taste

Instructions:

Prepare the Greens: Wash and dry both the basil and baby spinach leaves thoroughly.

Toast the Pine Nuts: In a dry skillet over medium-low heat, toast the pine nuts until lightly golden and fragrant. Stir frequently to prevent burning. Allow them to cool.

Crush the Garlic: Use a mortar and pestle to crush the peeled garlic cloves into a paste.

Combine Ingredients: In the mortar, add the basil leaves, baby spinach, toasted pine nuts, and crushed garlic. Begin gently grinding and crushing the ingredients together until you achieve a coarse paste.

Incorporate the Cheese: Gradually add the grated Parmesan cheese to the mortar and continue to grind and mix.

Drizzle in Olive Oil: While still grinding, slowly drizzle in the extra-virgin olive oil until the mixture becomes smooth and cohesive.

Season to Taste: Taste the pesto and season with salt and freshly ground black pepper according to your preference. Remember that the Parmesan cheese adds saltiness, so be cautious not to overdo it.

Serve and Enjoy: Your spinach and basil pesto is ready to be enjoyed! Pair it with your favorite pasta or use it as a sauce for other dishes.

Recipe 2: Arugula and Kale Pesto
Ingredients:

- 2 cups fresh arugula leaves, packed
- 2 cups fresh kale leaves, packed and stems removed

- 1/3 cup walnuts, toasted
- 2-3 cloves garlic, peeled
- 1/2 cup grated Pecorino or vegan Pecorino
- 1/2 cup extra-virgin olive oil
- Salt and freshly ground black pepper, to taste

Instructions:

Prepare the Greens: Wash and dry both the arugula and kale leaves thoroughly. Remove and discard the tough stems from the kale.

Toast the Walnuts: In a dry skillet over medium-low heat, toast the walnuts until lightly golden and fragrant. Stir frequently to prevent burning. Allow them to cool.

Crush the Garlic: Use a mortar and pestle to crush the peeled garlic cloves into a paste.

Combine Ingredients: In the mortar, add the arugula leaves, kale leaves, toasted walnuts, and crushed garlic. Begin gently grinding and crushing the ingredients together until you achieve a coarse paste.

Incorporate the Cheese: Gradually add the grated Pecorino cheese to the mortar and continue to grind and mix.

Drizzle in Olive Oil: While still grinding, slowly drizzle in the extra-virgin olive oil until the mixture becomes smooth and cohesive.

Season to Taste: Taste the pesto and season with salt and freshly ground black pepper according to your preference. Remember that the Pecorino cheese adds saltiness, so be cautious not to overdo it.

Serve and Enjoy: Your arugula and kale pesto is ready to be savored! It pairs wonderfully with whole-grain pasta, roasted vegetables, or grilled meats.

These wholesome green pesto recipes celebrate the diversity of leafy greens and their ability to enhance the flavor and nutrition of your pesto. Feel free to experiment with your favorite greens and discover new combinations that suit your palate.

Chapter 9: Sun-Kissed Bliss: Sun-Dried Tomatoes in Pesto

The Sweet and Tangy Appeal of Sun-Dried Tomatoes

Sun-dried tomatoes are culinary treasures that add a burst of sweet and tangy flavor to dishes, and when incorporated into pesto, they take the sauce to a whole new level of deliciousness. In this chapter, we'll explore the unique appeal of sun-dried tomatoes, discover various sun-dried tomato pesto variations, and prepare recipes that showcase the sun-kissed bliss of this remarkable ingredient.

The Allure of Sun-Dried Tomatoes

Sun-dried tomatoes are ripe tomatoes that have been dried in the sun or through dehydration. This process concentrates their flavors, resulting in a rich, sweet, and slightly tangy taste. Their chewy texture and intense flavor make them a fantastic addition to pesto, providing depth and complexity.

Sun-Dried Tomato Pesto Variations

Incorporating sun-dried tomatoes into your pesto opens up a world of flavor possibilities. You can experiment with different ingredients to create unique variations that suit your taste. Here are some sun-dried tomato pesto variations to consider:

1. Classic Sun-Dried Tomato Pesto:

- Flavor Profile: Sweet, tangy, and savory.
- Pairs Well With: Pasta, grilled chicken, sandwiches, and pizza.

Notes: This pesto is a rich and bold variation that combines the sweetness of sun-dried tomatoes with the freshness of basil.

2. Spicy Sun-Dried Tomato Pesto:

- Flavor Profile: Sweet, tangy, and spicy.
- Pairs Well With: Spicy pasta dishes, grilled shrimp, and as a

dipping sauce.

Notes: Add red pepper flakes or a touch of cayenne to give your pesto some heat, complementing the sun-dried tomato's sweetness.

3. Sun-Dried Tomato and Walnut Pesto:

- Flavor Profile: Sweet, nutty, and savory.
- Pairs Well With: Whole-grain pasta, roasted vegetables, and as a spread for sandwiches.

Notes: Walnuts add a delightful crunch and earthy flavor to this pesto.

4. Sun-Dried Tomato and Feta Pesto:

- Flavor Profile: Sweet, tangy, and creamy.
- Pairs Well With: Greek-inspired dishes, salads, and as a dip for pita bread.

Notes: The creamy texture of feta cheese complements the sun-dried tomatoes beautifully.

5. Sun-Dried Tomato and Basil Pesto:

- Flavor Profile: Sweet, tangy, and aromatic.
- Pairs Well With: Classic pasta dishes, bruschetta, and caprese salads.

Notes: This pesto highlights the harmonious marriage of sun-dried tomatoes and basil.

Recipes Highlighting Sun-Dried Tomatoes

Let's explore two enticing recipes that showcase the sun-kissed bliss of sun-dried tomato pesto.

Recipe 1: Classic Sun-Dried Tomato Pesto
Ingredients:

- 1 cup sun-dried tomatoes (dry, not in oil)
- 1/2 cup fresh basil leaves
- 1/2 cup grated Parmesan or vegan Parmesan
- 3 cloves garlic
- 1/2 cup extra-virgin olive oil
- Salt and freshly ground black pepper, to taste

Instructions:

Rehydrate the Sun-Dried Tomatoes: Place the sun-dried tomatoes in a bowl and cover them with hot water. Let them soak for about 15-20 minutes, or until they become soft. Drain and pat dry.

Combine Ingredients: In a food processor, combine the rehydrated sun-dried tomatoes, fresh basil leaves, grated Parmesan, garlic cloves, and a pinch of salt and black pepper.

Pulse and Blend: Pulse the ingredients in the food processor while gradually adding the extra-virgin olive oil. Continue to blend until the mixture reaches your desired consistency.

Taste and Adjust: Taste the pesto and adjust the seasoning with more salt and black pepper if needed.

Serve and Enjoy: Your classic sun-dried tomato pesto is ready to be enjoyed! It's perfect for tossing with pasta or using as a flavorful spread.

Recipe 2: Spicy Sun-Dried Tomato Pesto
Ingredients:

- 1 cup sun-dried tomatoes (dry, not in oil)
- 1/2 cup fresh basil leaves
- 1/2 cup grated Pecorino or vegan Pecorino
- 3 cloves garlic
- 1/4 teaspoon red pepper flakes (adjust to taste)
- 1/2 cup extra-virgin olive oil
- Salt, to taste

Instructions:

Rehydrate the Sun-Dried Tomatoes: Place the sun-dried tomatoes in a bowl and cover them with hot water. Let them soak for about 15-20 minutes, or until they become soft. Drain and pat dry.

Combine Ingredients: In a food processor, combine the rehydrated sun-dried tomatoes, fresh basil leaves, grated Pecorino, garlic cloves, and red pepper flakes.

Pulse and Blend: Pulse the ingredients in the food processor while gradually adding the extra-virgin olive oil. Continue to blend until the mixture reaches your desired consistency.

Taste and Adjust: Taste the pesto and adjust the seasoning with salt and more red pepper flakes if you desire more heat.

Serve and Enjoy: Your spicy sun-dried tomato pesto is ready to spice up your dishes! It's great for adding a kick to pasta, grilled meats, or sandwiches.

Sun-dried tomato pesto brings a burst of sweet, tangy, and savory flavors to your dishes, making it a versatile and delightful addition to your culinary repertoire. Feel free to customize these recipes to suit your taste and discover new ways to incorporate this sun-kissed bliss into your meals.

Chapter 10: Adding Creaminess: Creamy Pesto Variations

Embracing Creamy Textures in Pesto

While traditional pesto is known for its vibrant and herbaceous qualities, there's a whole world of creamy pesto variations that offer a lusciously smooth and velvety texture. Creamy pesto sauces are a delightful departure from the classic, and they bring a luxurious richness to your dishes. In this chapter, we'll explore the art of creating creamy pesto, delve into various recipe variations, and discover how to pair creamy pesto with pasta for a truly indulgent dining experience.

The Appeal of Creamy Pesto

Creamy pesto sauces offer a different dimension to the beloved pesto. By incorporating ingredients like cream, cheese, or even avocados, you can achieve a velvety texture that coats your pasta and other dishes luxuriously. The result is a creamy, comforting, and deeply satisfying sauce.

Creamy Pesto Recipe Variations

Creating creamy pesto is an opportunity to experiment with different ingredients and techniques. Here are some creamy pesto variations to consider:

1. Creamy Basil Pesto:

- Ingredients: Fresh basil, heavy cream, grated Parmesan, garlic, pine nuts, extra-virgin olive oil.
- Texture: Silky and rich, with a strong basil aroma.
- Pairs Well With: Linguine, fettuccine, or as a dipping sauce for bread.

2. Avocado Pesto:

- Ingredients: Avocado, fresh basil, lemon juice, garlic, grated

Parmesan, extra-virgin olive oil.
- Texture: Creamy and vibrant green, with a hint of citrus.
- Pairs Well With: Spiralized zucchini, grilled chicken, or as a dip for vegetables.

3. Creamy Sun-Dried Tomato Pesto:

- Ingredients: Sun-dried tomatoes, heavy cream, fresh basil, garlic, grated Parmesan, extra-virgin olive oil.
- Texture: Smooth and sun-kissed, with a sweet and tangy flavor.
- Pairs Well With: Penne pasta, grilled shrimp, or as a spread for sandwiches.

4. Ricotta and Spinach Pesto:

- Ingredients: Ricotta cheese, fresh spinach, garlic, grated Pecorino, pine nuts, extra-virgin olive oil.
- Texture: Velvety and vibrant green, with a mild ricotta creaminess.
- Pairs Well With: Farfalle pasta, roasted vegetables, or as a topping for baked potatoes.

5. Creamy Roasted Red Pepper Pesto:

- Ingredients: Roasted red peppers, heavy cream, fresh basil, garlic, grated Parmesan, extra-virgin olive oil.
- Texture: Silky and vibrant orange, with a smoky sweetness.
- Pairs Well With: Rigatoni pasta, grilled steak, or as a dip for breadsticks.

Pairing Creamy Pesto with Pasta

Creamy pesto and pasta are a match made in culinary heaven. The silky, velvety sauce clings to the pasta, creating a luxurious and comforting dish. Here's a simple guide to pairing creamy pesto with pasta:

Linguine: Long, flat linguine noodles are perfect for creamy basil pesto or avocado pesto. The creamy sauce coats the noodles beautifully.

Fettuccine: Wide fettuccine ribbons are a great choice for creamy pesto, especially if you're using spinach or sun-dried tomato variations. The broad surface area allows for maximum sauce coverage.

Penne: Penne pasta's ridges and tubular shape are excellent for capturing creamy pesto. It's an ideal choice for sun-dried tomato or roasted red pepper pesto.

Farfalle: Bowtie-shaped farfalle pasta pairs wonderfully with ricotta and spinach pesto. The nooks and crannies of the pasta hold onto the creamy sauce.

Rigatoni: The large, ridged tubes of rigatoni pasta are perfect for creamy pesto with a rich texture, such as creamy roasted red pepper pesto.

Recipe: Creamy Basil Pesto Pasta

Ingredients:

- 12 ounces linguine pasta
- 1 batch creamy basil pesto
- Grated Parmesan cheese, for garnish
- Fresh basil leaves, for garnish
- Cherry tomatoes, halved, for garnish (optional)

Instructions:

Cook the Pasta: Bring a large pot of salted water to a boil. Cook the linguine pasta according to the package instructions until al dente. Drain and set aside.

Prepare the Creamy Basil Pesto: Prepare a batch of creamy basil pesto using the ingredients and instructions provided in the creamy basil pesto variation.

Combine Pasta and Pesto: In a large mixing bowl, toss the cooked linguine with the creamy basil pesto until well coated.

Garnish and Serve: Plate the creamy basil pesto pasta and garnish with grated Parmesan cheese, fresh basil leaves, and halved cherry tomatoes if desired.

Enjoy: Serve immediately and enjoy the creamy, herbaceous goodness of this dish.

Creamy pesto pasta dishes are perfect for special occasions, date nights, or anytime you crave a comforting yet indulgent meal. Feel free to experiment with different creamy pesto variations and pasta shapes to discover your favorite combinations.

Chapter 11: Spicy Surprises: Pesto with a Kick

Igniting Flavor with Spicy Elements

For those who crave a little heat in their meals, spicy pesto is a tantalizing option that elevates the classic sauce to a whole new level. By infusing pesto with fiery elements, you can ignite your taste buds and add a delightful kick to your dishes. In this chapter, we'll explore the art of creating spicy pesto, discover various sources of heat, and unveil bold and spicy pesto recipes that will awaken your palate.

The Allure of Spicy Pesto

Spicy pesto is a flavor-packed departure from the traditional sauce, and it brings a fiery zest to your dishes. Whether you prefer a subtle warmth or a blazing inferno, there are numerous ways to incorporate spicy elements into pesto, from chili peppers to spicy oils and condiments.

Exploring Heat Sources for Pesto

To create spicy pesto, you can explore a range of heat sources to suit your taste preferences. Here are some options:

1. Chili Peppers:

- Varieties: Choose from mild to scorching options like jalapeños, serranos, habaneros, or ghost peppers.
- Texture: Fresh chili peppers can add both heat and texture to your pesto, while dried chili flakes offer uniform spiciness.

2. Spicy Oils:

- Types: Infuse your pesto with chili oil, sriracha-infused oil, or other spicy oils available.
- Texture: Spicy oils blend seamlessly into the sauce, providing even distribution of heat.

3. Hot Sauces:

- Varieties: Experiment with different hot sauces, from smoky chipotle to fiery Scotch bonnet.
- Texture: Hot sauces are liquid and blend smoothly into pesto, allowing you to control the level of heat.

4. Spicy Condiments:

- Options: Include ingredients like harissa paste, gochujang, or sambal oelek for unique spicy flavors.
- Texture: Spicy condiments provide both heat and depth to your pesto.

5. Dried Spices:

- Varieties: Add ground spices like cayenne pepper, red pepper flakes, or smoked paprika for controlled spiciness.
- Texture: Dried spices blend easily and evenly into the pesto.

Bold and Spicy Pesto Recipes

Let's explore two bold and spicy pesto recipes that will awaken your taste buds.

Recipe 1: Spicy Basil and Jalapeño Pesto
Ingredients:

- 2 cups fresh basil leaves, packed
- 2-3 jalapeño peppers, seeds removed (adjust to desired spice level)
- 2-3 cloves garlic, peeled
- 1/2 cup grated Parmesan or vegan Parmesan
- 1/2 cup extra-virgin olive oil
- Salt and freshly ground black pepper, to taste

Instructions:
Prepare the Basil: Wash and dry the basil leaves thoroughly.

Prepare the Jalapeños: Remove the seeds and membranes from the jalapeño peppers to control the heat. If you prefer a milder pesto, use only one jalapeño.

Combine Ingredients: In a food processor, combine the basil leaves, jalapeño peppers, peeled garlic cloves, and a pinch of salt and black pepper.

Pulse and Blend: Pulse the ingredients in the food processor while gradually adding the extra-virgin olive oil. Continue to blend until the mixture reaches your desired consistency.

Incorporate the Cheese: Gradually add the grated Parmesan cheese to the food processor and blend until the pesto is smooth and well combined.

Taste and Adjust: Taste the pesto and adjust the seasoning with more salt and black pepper if needed.

Serve and Enjoy: Your spicy basil and jalapeño pesto is ready to spice up your dishes! Pair it with pasta, grilled shrimp, or as a dipping sauce.

Recipe 2: Smoky Chipotle Pesto
Ingredients:

- 2 cups fresh cilantro leaves, packed
- 1-2 chipotle peppers in adobo sauce (adjust to desired spice level)
- 2-3 cloves garlic, peeled
- 1/2 cup grated Pecorino or vegan Pecorino
- 1/2 cup extra-virgin olive oil
- Salt and freshly ground black pepper, to taste

Instructions:
Prepare the Cilantro: Wash and dry the cilantro leaves thoroughly.

Prepare the Chipotle Peppers: Remove the chipotle peppers from the adobo sauce and discard the seeds for milder heat. Use more or less chipotle peppers based on your desired spice level.

Combine Ingredients: In a food processor, combine the cilantro leaves, chipotle peppers, peeled garlic cloves, and a pinch of salt and black pepper.

Pulse and Blend: Pulse the ingredients in the food processor while gradually adding the extra-virgin olive oil. Continue to blend until the mixture reaches your desired consistency.

Incorporate the Cheese: Gradually add the grated Pecorino cheese to the food processor and blend until the pesto is smooth and well combined.

Taste and Adjust: Taste the pesto and adjust the seasoning with more salt and black pepper if needed.

Serve and Enjoy: Your smoky chipotle pesto is ready to add a fiery smokiness to your dishes! It pairs wonderfully with pasta, grilled meats, or as a spread for sandwiches.

Spicy pesto recipes bring excitement and bold flavors to your meals, allowing you to customize the level of heat to your liking. Whether you prefer the lively kick of jalapeños or the smoky allure of chipotle peppers, these pesto variations are sure to satisfy your craving for spice.

Chapter 12: The Art of Pairing: Matching Pesto with Pasta Shapes

Pesto and Pasta: A Match Made in Heaven

The beauty of pesto lies in its versatility, and one of the most delightful pairings for pesto is pasta. The way the sauce coats the pasta shapes, creating a harmonious blend of flavors and textures, is a culinary symphony. In this chapter, we'll explore the art of pairing pesto with various pasta shapes, providing you with tips and inspiration for achieving pasta-pesto harmony that will elevate your dining experience.

The Perfect Pairing

Pesto and pasta are a timeless duo that transcends culinary boundaries. The herbaceous, nutty, or spicy notes of pesto complement the texture and form of different pasta shapes, creating a symphony of flavors and sensations. The key to a perfect pairing is understanding which pasta shape complements the specific pesto you're using.

Pairing Pesto with Various Pasta Shapes

Let's delve into the world of pasta and pesto pairings, highlighting some classic and creative combinations:

1. Spaghetti:

- Pesto Pairings: Classic Genovese pesto, basil pesto, creamy pesto variations.
- Why It Works: Spaghetti's long, slender shape allows the sauce to cling beautifully, creating a harmonious bite.

2. Fettuccine:

- Pesto Pairings: Creamy pesto variations, mushroom pesto, sun-dried tomato pesto.

- Why It Works: The broad ribbons of fettuccine capture the creamy sauce, ensuring each bite is rich and satisfying.

3. Farfalle (Bowtie):

- Pesto Pairings: Creamy spinach pesto, ricotta and spinach pesto, walnut pesto.
- Why It Works: Farfalle's nooks and crannies hold onto creamy and chunky pesto variations, creating a delightful texture.

4. Penne:

- Pesto Pairings: Classic basil pesto, sun-dried tomato pesto, spicy pesto.
- Why It Works: Penne's tubular shape captures chunky pesto elements, and its ridges hold onto the sauce, ensuring a flavorful bite.

5. Orzo:

- Pesto Pairings: Lemon zest and herb pesto, arugula pesto, pesto with a kick.
- Why It Works: Orzo's small size and rice-like shape pair beautifully with lighter, citrusy pesto variations.

6. Rotini:

- Pesto Pairings: Pesto with roasted nuts, creamy roasted red pepper pesto, smoky chipotle pesto.
- Why It Works: Rotini's spiraled form captures both creamy and chunky pesto, offering a flavorful and textural experience.

7. Orecchiette:

- Pesto Pairings: Pesto with leafy greens, avocado pesto, spicy jalapeño pesto.
- Why It Works: Orecchiette's bowl-like shape cradles pesto with leafy greens or chunky textures perfectly.

8. Cavatappi:

- Pesto Pairings: Artichoke and spinach pesto, pesto with sun-dried tomatoes, pesto with a kick.
- Why It Works: Cavatappi's ridges and hollow center capture chunky pesto elements, creating a delightful bite.

Tips for Achieving Pasta-Pesto Harmony

Achieving the perfect pasta-pesto harmony is an art, and here are some tips to ensure your dish sings with flavor:

Cook Pasta Al Dente: Cook your pasta al dente (firm to the bite) to create a pleasing contrast with the creamy or chunky pesto.

Reserve Pasta Water: Before draining the pasta, save some of the cooking water. It contains starch that can help thicken and emulsify the pesto sauce when mixed.

Combine Gradually: Add the pesto to the drained pasta gradually, tossing and mixing as you go. This ensures an even coating.

Adjust Consistency: If your pesto is too thick, use a bit of the reserved pasta water to thin it out. Conversely, if it's too thin, add more cheese, nuts, or herbs to thicken it.

Garnish Wisely: Garnish your pasta-pesto dish with fresh herbs, grated cheese, or toasted nuts for added texture and flavor.

Experiment and Enjoy: Don't be afraid to experiment with different pasta shapes and pesto variations to discover your favorite combinations.

Pairing pesto with pasta shapes is an art that allows you to create a symphony of flavors and textures on your plate. Whether you're savoring a classic pairing or exploring creative combinations, the result is always a delightful culinary experience.

Chapter 13: Pesto Pizzazz: Creative Uses Beyond Pasta

Pesto Beyond the Spaghetti Bowl

While pesto is undeniably a pasta superstar, its versatility extends far beyond the world of pasta. In this chapter, we'll explore the exciting and creative applications of pesto in a variety of dishes, from appetizers and sandwiches to salads and protein-based meals. Discover how pesto can be a flavor booster, elevating your culinary creations to new heights.

A World of Pesto Possibilities

Pesto is a flavor-packed sauce that can transform even the simplest dishes into culinary delights. Its vibrant green color and herbaceous, nutty, or spicy flavors make it a versatile ingredient that enhances a wide range of recipes.

Creative Applications of Pesto

Let's dive into some creative uses of pesto that go beyond pasta:

1. Pesto Pizza:

Spread pesto as the base sauce for homemade pizzas. Top with your favorite ingredients like mozzarella, cherry tomatoes, and fresh basil for a burst of flavor.

2. Pesto-Stuffed Mushrooms:

Fill mushroom caps with a mixture of pesto, cream cheese, and breadcrumbs. Bake until golden for a savory appetizer.

3. Pesto Potato Salad:

Toss boiled potatoes with pesto, cherry tomatoes, red onion, and a touch of mayonnaise for a refreshing side dish.

4. Pesto Caprese Skewers:

Thread mozzarella balls, cherry tomatoes, and basil leaves onto skewers. Drizzle with pesto for a quick and elegant appetizer.

5. Pesto-Stuffed Chicken Breast:

Slice a pocket into chicken breasts and stuff with pesto and mozzarella. Bake until the chicken is cooked through and the cheese is melted.

6. Pesto Grilled Cheese:

Spread pesto between slices of bread along with your favorite cheese for a gourmet grilled cheese sandwich.

7. Pesto Veggie Wraps:

Use large lettuce leaves as wraps and fill them with sliced vegetables, grilled chicken, and a drizzle of pesto.

8. Pesto Quinoa Salad:

Mix cooked quinoa with pesto, roasted vegetables, and feta cheese for a hearty and flavorful salad.

9. Pesto Deviled Eggs:

Add a dollop of pesto to the yolk mixture of deviled eggs for a unique twist on a classic appetizer.

10. Pesto Tofu Skewers:

Marinate cubes of tofu in pesto, then thread them onto skewers with bell peppers and onions. Grill for a tasty vegetarian dish.

Pesto as a Flavor Booster

Pesto isn't just a sauce; it's a flavor booster that can enhance a wide range of dishes. Here are some tips for using pesto to elevate your culinary creations:

Marinades: Use pesto as a marinade for meats, poultry, or seafood. It infuses them with herbaceous and nutty flavors before cooking.

Dips and Spreads: Create flavorful dips and spreads by combining pesto with cream cheese, Greek yogurt, or hummus. Serve with crackers, bread, or fresh vegetables.

Salad Dressing: Transform ordinary salads into extraordinary ones by drizzling pesto mixed with olive oil and vinegar over your greens.

Soup Enhancer: Stir a spoonful of pesto into your favorite soups, whether it's tomato, minestrone, or vegetable soup, for a burst of flavor.

Potato Dishes: Pesto pairs beautifully with potatoes. Add it to mashed potatoes, roasted potatoes, or even potato salad.

Burger Topping: Elevate your burgers by spreading pesto on the buns before assembling. It adds a burst of flavor and keeps the burger moist.

Egg Dishes: Whether it's scrambled eggs, omelets, or a frittata, swirl pesto into your egg dishes for a savory kick.

Pesto's versatility knows no bounds, and it can transform ordinary meals into culinary masterpieces. Get creative in the kitchen and explore the endless possibilities of this vibrant sauce.

Chapter 14: Mediterranean Flavors: Pesto in Mediterranean Cuisine

Pesto's Connection to Mediterranean Cuisine

Pesto, with its vibrant herbaceous flavors and rich history, shares a deep-rooted connection with Mediterranean cuisine. In this chapter, we'll explore the synergy between pesto and Mediterranean culinary traditions. From Greece to Italy to the shores of North Africa, discover how pesto is used as an ingredient and a source of inspiration in creating mouthwatering Mediterranean dishes.

A Mediterranean Affair

Mediterranean cuisine is known for its emphasis on fresh ingredients, bold flavors, and healthful eating. Pesto, with its core components of fresh herbs, olive oil, and nuts, perfectly aligns with the principles of Mediterranean cooking.

Mediterranean-Inspired Pesto Recipes

Let's embark on a culinary journey through Mediterranean-inspired pesto recipes that showcase the vibrant flavors of this region:

1. Greek Pesto:

- Ingredients: Fresh oregano and mint, Kalamata olives, feta cheese, garlic, extra-virgin olive oil, pine nuts.
- Flavor Profile: Herbaceous, briny, and savory.
- Pairing Suggestions: Toss with orzo pasta, serve over grilled lamb, or use as a dip for pita bread.

2. Mediterranean Sundried Tomato Pesto:

- Ingredients: Sun-dried tomatoes, fresh basil, garlic, almonds, extra-virgin olive oil, red pepper flakes.
- Flavor Profile: Sweet, tangy, and slightly spicy.
- Pairing Suggestions: Serve with roasted vegetables, spread on

crostini, or mix with cooked couscous.

3. Moroccan-Inspired Pesto:

- Ingredients: Cilantro, mint, preserved lemon, almonds, cumin, coriander, extra-virgin olive oil.
- Flavor Profile: Bright, zesty, and aromatic.
- Pairing Suggestions: Drizzle over grilled chicken, use as a marinade for seafood, or toss with couscous and chickpeas.

4. Italian-Middle Eastern Fusion Pesto:

- Ingredients: Fresh basil, parsley, tahini, pine nuts, lemon juice, garlic, extra-virgin olive oil.
- Flavor Profile: Creamy, nutty, and slightly tangy.
- Pairing Suggestions: Serve as a dip with falafel, spread on flatbreads, or toss with pasta and grilled vegetables.

Incorporating Pesto into Mediterranean Dishes

Pesto can be a versatile addition to Mediterranean dishes, enhancing their flavors and adding a touch of vibrancy. Here are some ways to incorporate pesto into Mediterranean cuisine:

Mediterranean Grain Salads: Mix pesto with cooked grains like quinoa, bulgur, or couscous. Add chopped vegetables, olives, and feta cheese for a refreshing salad.

Mediterranean Mezze Platter: Serve pesto as one of the dips on a mezze platter alongside hummus, tzatziki, and baba ganoush. It pairs well with fresh pita bread and an assortment of veggies.

Grilled Seafood: Brush pesto onto grilled fish or shrimp for a burst of flavor. The herbaceous notes of pesto complement the natural flavors of seafood beautifully.

Mediterranean Sandwiches: Spread pesto on sandwiches or wraps filled with Mediterranean ingredients like roasted vegetables, grilled chicken, or falafel.

Mediterranean Pasta Dishes: Toss cooked pasta with pesto and Mediterranean ingredients such as cherry tomatoes, artichoke hearts, and feta cheese.

Pesto's versatility and Mediterranean roots make it a delightful addition to dishes inspired by this region. By infusing pesto into your Mediterranean cooking, you can elevate familiar dishes and create exciting new flavors.

Chapter 15: Globetrotter's Pesto: International Pesto Adventures

Pesto Around the World

Pesto, with its versatility and captivating flavors, transcends borders and has found its way into cuisines around the world. In this chapter, we'll embark on an international culinary adventure, exploring pesto variations and traditions from different corners of the globe. From South America to Asia, discover how pesto has evolved and adapted to the tastes and ingredients of diverse cultures.

A World of Pesto

Pesto's global appeal is a testament to its ability to harmonize with a wide range of ingredients and culinary traditions. As it travels from one continent to another, it takes on new flavors and characteristics, resulting in a rich tapestry of international pesto variations.

International Pesto Variations

Let's take a flavorful journey through international pesto variations:

1. Brazilian Pesto (Molho à Campanha):

- Ingredients: Tomatoes, bell peppers, onions, parsley, garlic, olive oil, vinegar.
- Flavor Profile: Fresh, zesty, and slightly tangy.
- Pairing Suggestions: Serve as a condiment for grilled meats, especially churrasco-style barbecue.

2. Thai-Inspired Pesto:

- Ingredients: Thai basil, cilantro, peanuts, garlic, lime juice, fish sauce.
- Flavor Profile: Herbaceous, nutty, and tangy with a hint of heat.
- Pairing Suggestions: Toss with rice noodles and shrimp or use as a dipping sauce for spring rolls.

3. Argentinian Chimichurri:

- Ingredients: Parsley, oregano, garlic, red pepper flakes, red wine vinegar, olive oil.
- Flavor Profile: Vibrant, garlicky, and slightly spicy.
- Pairing Suggestions: Drizzle over grilled steaks, chicken, or vegetables.

4. Japanese-Style Pesto:

- Ingredients: Shiso leaves, toasted sesame seeds, miso paste, mirin, rice vinegar.
- Flavor Profile: Nutty, umami-rich, and slightly sweet.
- Pairing Suggestions: Use as a dipping sauce for sushi or sashimi, or toss with cold soba noodles.

5. Mexican Poblano Pesto:

- Ingredients: Roasted poblano peppers, cilantro, cotija cheese, pumpkin seeds, lime juice.
- Flavor Profile: Smoky, earthy, and mildly spicy.
- Pairing Suggestions: Serve with tacos, grilled corn, or as a topping for enchiladas.

Exploring Global Pesto Traditions

Pesto has a way of adapting to local ingredients and cultural preferences, creating unique traditions in each corner of the world. Here are some insights into global pesto traditions:

Argentina: Chimichurri is a beloved sauce, typically served with grilled meats. It combines parsley, oregano, and garlic with a tangy kick from red wine vinegar.

Brazil: Molho à Campanha is a Brazilian salsa-like sauce that features fresh tomatoes, bell peppers, and onions. It adds a burst of freshness to grilled meats.

Japan: Japanese-style pesto often incorporates shiso leaves, a fragrant herb, along with miso paste and sesame seeds. It's used to flavor sushi, sashimi, and noodle dishes.

Thailand: Thai-inspired pesto combines the vibrant flavors of Thai basil, cilantro, peanuts, and lime juice. It's a delightful companion to Thai cuisine, especially noodle dishes.

Mexico: Poblano pesto highlights the smoky and slightly spicy notes of roasted poblano peppers. It's a versatile condiment for Mexican-inspired dishes.

Global pesto traditions showcase the adaptability of this sauce and how it can enhance the flavors of various cuisines. As you explore these international pesto variations, you'll gain a deeper appreciation for the diverse culinary landscapes of the world.

Chapter 16: Vegan and Dairy-Free Delights

Embracing Vegan and Dairy-Free Pesto

Pesto's adaptability extends to dietary preferences, including vegan and dairy-free options. In this chapter, we'll explore the world of plant-based pesto, which retains all the flavors and textures of traditional pesto while embracing vegan and dairy-free ingredients. Discover how to create delectable pesto sauces that cater to a vegan and dairy-free lifestyle.

A World of Vegan Pesto

Vegan and dairy-free pesto is a testament to culinary creativity. By substituting traditional cheese and dairy ingredients with plant-based alternatives, you can enjoy the vibrant flavors of pesto while staying true to your dietary choices.

Vegan Cheese Substitutes and Alternatives

Before we dive into plant-based pesto recipes, let's explore some vegan cheese substitutes and alternatives that can be used to recreate the creamy and cheesy elements of traditional pesto:

Nutritional Yeast: This deactivated yeast has a cheesy, umami flavor and is often used to mimic the taste of Parmesan cheese.

Vegan Parmesan: You can find vegan Parmesan cheese in stores or make your own by blending nuts, nutritional yeast, garlic powder, and salt.

Cashews: Soaked and blended cashews can create a creamy texture in vegan pesto recipes.

Almonds: Blanched almonds, when soaked and blended, can add a creamy and slightly sweet quality to vegan pesto.

Tofu: Silken tofu is a versatile ingredient that can be used to create a creamy base for vegan pesto.

Vegan Cream Cheese: Plant-based cream cheese alternatives can add creaminess and tanginess to your pesto.

Now, let's explore some delicious plant-based pesto recipes:

Plant-Based Pesto Recipes

1. Classic Vegan Pesto:

- Ingredients: Fresh basil, garlic, pine nuts, nutritional yeast, extra-virgin olive oil, lemon juice, salt, and pepper.
- Flavor Profile: Herbaceous, nutty, and slightly tangy.
- Pairing Suggestions: Toss with pasta, use as a spread on sandwiches, or drizzle over roasted vegetables.

2. Creamy Cashew Pesto:

- Ingredients: Fresh basil, garlic, soaked cashews, nutritional yeast, lemon juice, extra-virgin olive oil, salt, and pepper.
- Flavor Profile: Creamy, nutty, and slightly tangy.
- Pairing Suggestions: Serve with spiralized zucchini noodles, use as a dip for bread, or spread on pizza crust.

3. Sunflower Seed Pesto:

- Ingredients: Fresh basil, garlic, sunflower seeds, nutritional yeast, lemon juice, extra-virgin olive oil, salt, and pepper.
- Flavor Profile: Nutty, slightly tangy, and subtly sweet.
- Pairing Suggestions: Toss with whole wheat pasta, mix into grain salads, or use as a dressing for roasted vegetables.

4. Vegan Spinach and Walnut Pesto:

- Ingredients: Baby spinach, garlic, walnuts, nutritional yeast, lemon juice, extra-virgin olive oil, salt, and pepper.
- Flavor Profile: Earthy, slightly nutty, and refreshing.
- Pairing Suggestions: Serve with gnocchi, spread on sandwiches, or use as a dip for vegetable sticks.

5. Tofu and Herb Pesto:

- Ingredients: Fresh herbs (e.g., basil, parsley, cilantro), garlic, silken tofu, nutritional yeast, lemon juice, extra-virgin olive oil, salt, and pepper.
- Flavor Profile: Bright, herbaceous, and creamy.
- Pairing Suggestions: Toss with rice noodles, use as a marinade for tofu, or drizzle over grilled vegetables.

Vegan and dairy-free pesto opens up a world of delicious possibilities for those with dietary preferences and restrictions. These plant-based pesto recipes allow you to savor the flavors and textures of pesto while staying true to your vegan and dairy-free lifestyle.

Chapter 17: Pesto for Every Season

Seasonal Pesto Creations

Pesto is a sauce that thrives on the freshest seasonal ingredients, celebrating the flavors of each season. In this chapter, we'll take you on a culinary journey through the four seasons, showcasing pesto recipes that are perfectly tailored to the produce and moods of spring, summer, fall, and winter. Discover how to savor the essence of each season with vibrant and flavorful pesto creations.

The Seasonal Pesto Palette

Each season brings its unique bounty of fresh herbs, vegetables, and fruits. By harnessing the power of seasonal ingredients, you can create pesto sauces that reflect the spirit of the time of year.

Spring Pesto Recipes

Spring Vegetable Pesto:

- Ingredients: Fresh peas, asparagus, mint, garlic, pine nuts, Parmesan cheese, extra-virgin olive oil, lemon zest, salt, and pepper.
- Flavor Profile: Bright, herbaceous, and subtly sweet.
- Pairing Suggestions: Toss with spring pasta, drizzle over grilled chicken, or use as a dip for crudité.

Strawberry Basil Pesto:

- Ingredients: Fresh strawberries, basil, almonds, garlic, goat cheese, extra-virgin olive oil, balsamic vinegar, salt, and pepper.
- Flavor Profile: Sweet, fruity, and herbaceous.
- Pairing Suggestions: Serve with grilled halloumi cheese, spread on crostini, or use as a topping for a spinach salad.

Summer Pesto Recipes

Caprese Pesto:

- Ingredients: Fresh basil, cherry tomatoes, fresh mozzarella, garlic, pine nuts, extra-virgin olive oil, balsamic glaze, salt, and pepper.
- Flavor Profile: Fresh, tangy, and herbaceous.
- Pairing Suggestions: Layer with ripe tomatoes and drizzle with balsamic glaze for a Caprese salad, spread on grilled baguette slices, or toss with cooked pasta.

Grilled Peach and Arugula Pesto:

- Ingredients: Grilled peaches, arugula, almonds, garlic, Pecorino cheese, extra-virgin olive oil, lemon juice, salt, and pepper.
- Flavor Profile: Sweet, peppery, and slightly nutty.
- Pairing Suggestions: Serve with grilled pork chops, spread on flatbreads, or toss with quinoa and roasted vegetables.

Fall Pesto Recipes

Butternut Sage Pesto:

- Ingredients: Roasted butternut squash, fresh sage, walnuts, garlic, Parmesan cheese, extra-virgin olive oil, nutmeg, salt, and pepper.
- Flavor Profile: Earthy, nutty, and warmly spiced.
- Pairing Suggestions: Toss with gnocchi, spread on a turkey sandwich, or use as a topping for roasted Brussels sprouts.

Apple and Rosemary Pesto:

- Ingredients: Fresh apples, rosemary, pecans, garlic, Cheddar cheese, extra-virgin olive oil, apple cider vinegar, salt, and

pepper.
- Flavor Profile: Sweet, savory, and aromatic.
- Pairing Suggestions: Serve with roasted chicken, spread on whole-grain crackers, or mix into a kale salad.

Winter Pesto Recipes
Kale and Walnut Pesto:

- Ingredients: Lacinato kale, toasted walnuts, garlic, Parmesan cheese, extra-virgin olive oil, lemon juice, red pepper flakes, salt, and pepper.
- Flavor Profile: Robust, nutty, and slightly spicy.
- Pairing Suggestions: Toss with whole wheat pasta, spread on a turkey burger, or mix into mashed potatoes.

Roasted Beet Pesto:

- Ingredients: Roasted beets, fresh dill, pistachios, garlic, feta cheese, extra-virgin olive oil, red wine vinegar, salt, and pepper.
- Flavor Profile: Earthy, herbaceous, and slightly tangy.
- Pairing Suggestions: Serve with grilled lamb, spread on rye bread, or use as a topping for roasted root vegetables.

Preserving the Freshness of Each Season
To capture the essence of each season, consider preserving pesto in various ways:

Freezing: Freeze pesto in ice cube trays or small containers for easy portioning. Thaw as needed and enjoy a taste of the season all year round.

Canning: Preserve pesto in jars using a water bath canning method to enjoy homemade pesto even during the off-season.

Dehydrating: Make pesto powder by dehydrating pesto and then grinding it into a fine powder. Rehydrate with olive oil when needed.

Vacuum Sealing: Use a vacuum sealer to store pesto in airtight bags, keeping it fresh for an extended period.

Embracing the flavors of each season through pesto creations is a delightful way to experience the changing culinary landscape throughout the year. Whether you're savoring the freshness of spring or the cozy comfort of winter, seasonal pesto recipes offer a taste of nature's bounty in every bite.

Chapter 18: Pesto Party: Hosting Pesto-Themed Gatherings

Hosting a Pesto Party: Tips and Ideas

Pesto lovers unite! Hosting a pesto-themed gathering is a wonderful way to share your love for this vibrant sauce with friends and family. In this chapter, we'll provide you with tips, ideas, and inspiration for hosting a memorable pesto party. From decor to menu planning, we've got you covered.

The Pesto Party Experience

A pesto party is all about celebrating the flavors and versatility of this beloved sauce. Whether it's a casual backyard barbecue, an elegant dinner party, or a relaxed weekend brunch, there are endless possibilities for crafting the perfect pesto-themed gathering.

Pesto Party Menus and Themes

Let's explore some delightful pesto party menu ideas and themes that will impress your guests and make your gathering a memorable one:

1. Pasta Extravaganza:

Pesto Pasta Bar: Set up a pasta bar with various pasta shapes and types, a selection of homemade pesto sauces, and an array of toppings like grilled chicken, sautéed mushrooms, cherry tomatoes, and grated cheese. Let guests create their personalized pesto pasta dishes.

Pesto-Stuffed Pastries: Serve flaky puff pastry bites stuffed with pesto and cheese for appetizers.

2. Mediterranean Pesto Fiesta:

Mediterranean Mezze Platter: Create a vibrant mezze platter featuring hummus, tzatziki, baba ganoush, olives, pita bread, and a refreshing Mediterranean pesto dip.

Pesto-Infused Seafood: Grill or roast seafood with a Mediterranean twist by brushing it with pesto before cooking.

3. Backyard BBQ with Pesto Flair:

Pesto Burgers: Offer grilled burgers topped with pesto and mozzarella, along with classic BBQ sides.

Pesto Potato Salad: Elevate the potato salad with a creamy pesto dressing.

4. Pesto and Pizza Party:

Make-Your-Own Pesto Pizzas: Set up a DIY pizza station with pizza dough, a variety of pesto sauces, cheese, and toppings. Let guests assemble and bake their pesto pizzas.

Pesto Garlic Knots: Serve garlic knots brushed with pesto for a tasty appetizer.

5. Brunch with a Pesto Twist:

Pesto Omelets: Offer a build-your-own omelet station with pesto, a variety of veggies, cheeses, and proteins.

Pesto Avocado Toast: Elevate avocado toast by spreading pesto on the bread before topping with avocado slices.

Pesto Cocktails and Mocktails

No pesto party is complete without some refreshing beverages. Here are some pesto-inspired cocktail and mocktail ideas to quench your guests' thirst:

1. Pesto Martini:

- Ingredients: Gin, dry vermouth, a splash of homemade basil pesto, ice, fresh basil leaves for garnish.
- Instructions: Shake gin, vermouth, and pesto with ice. Strain into a martini glass and garnish with fresh basil leaves.

2. Pesto Lemonade Spritzer (Mocktail):

- Ingredients: Lemonade, soda water, a splash of homemade lemon basil pesto, ice, lemon slices for garnish.
- Instructions: Mix lemonade, soda water, and pesto in a glass with ice. Garnish with lemon slices.

3. Pesto Bloody Mary:

- Ingredients: Vodka, tomato juice, pesto, Worcestershire sauce, hot sauce, lemon juice, ice, celery stalk and cherry tomatoes for garnish.
- Instructions: Combine vodka, tomato juice, pesto, Worcestershire sauce, hot sauce, and lemon juice in a shaker with ice. Shake and strain into a glass. Garnish with celery and cherry tomatoes.

4. Pesto Mojito (Mocktail):

- Ingredients: Lime juice, mint leaves, simple syrup, a splash of homemade basil pesto, soda water, ice, lime wedges for garnish.
- Instructions: Muddle lime juice, mint leaves, and simple syrup in a glass. Add pesto, ice, and top with soda water. Garnish with lime wedges.

5. Pesto Sangria:

- Ingredients: Red wine, pesto, orange liqueur, lemon juice, assorted fruits (e.g., oranges, apples, berries), ice.
- Instructions: Combine red wine, pesto, orange liqueur, and lemon juice in a pitcher. Add sliced fruits and refrigerate for at least an hour. Serve over ice.

Hosting a pesto party is a flavorful and fun way to bring people together and celebrate the versatility of this beloved sauce. Whether you choose a specific theme or simply indulge in an array of pesto dishes, your guests are sure to leave with happy taste buds and fond memories.

Chapter 19: Homemade vs. Store-Bought: The Pesto Dilemma

Homemade Pesto vs. Store-Bought Options

The age-old question when it comes to pesto: should you make it from scratch or opt for the convenience of store-bought options? In this chapter, we'll dive deep into the homemade vs. store-bought pesto dilemma, exploring the pros and cons of each, and providing you with insights on how to choose quality store-bought pesto when needed.

Pesto: To DIY or Not to DIY

Pesto is a versatile sauce that can be enjoyed in various dishes, and the decision between homemade and store-bought pesto depends on your preferences, time constraints, and culinary goals.

Pros and Cons of Homemade Pesto

Pros:

1. Full Control Over Ingredients:

Homemade pesto allows you to choose the freshest and highest-quality ingredients, ensuring that the sauce is tailored to your taste.

2. Endless Customization:

You have the creative freedom to experiment with different herbs, nuts, and cheeses, creating unique pesto variations.

3. Freshness and Flavor:

Nothing compares to the vibrant, freshly made flavor of homemade pesto. The aroma and taste are unparalleled.

4. No Preservatives or Additives:

Homemade pesto is free from artificial preservatives or additives, making it a healthier option.

Cons:

1. Time-Consuming:

Making pesto from scratch can be time-consuming, especially if you're preparing a large batch.

2. Ingredient Sourcing:

Finding high-quality ingredients, especially if you're growing your own herbs, can be a challenge.

3. Seasonal Availability:

Some key pesto ingredients, like fresh basil, may not be readily available year-round.

4. Short Shelf Life:

Homemade pesto typically has a shorter shelf life compared to store-bought options.

Pros and Cons of Store-Bought Pesto

Pros:

1. Convenience:

Store-bought pesto is convenient, requiring no prep work or cooking. It's ready to use.

2. Long Shelf Life:

Commercially produced pesto has a longer shelf life, allowing for pantry storage.

3. Consistency:

Store-bought pesto maintains a consistent flavor and texture, ensuring a reliable taste.

4. Variety:

You can find a variety of store-bought pesto options, including traditional, vegan, and unique flavor profiles.

Cons:

1. Preservatives:

Some store-bought pesto brands may contain preservatives and additives to prolong shelf life.

2. Limited Customization:

Store-bought options offer less flexibility in terms of customizing flavors to your preference.

3. Quality Variation:

The quality of store-bought pesto can vary widely among brands, and some may not meet your taste expectations.

How to Choose Quality Store-Bought Pesto

When opting for store-bought pesto, follow these tips to ensure you select a high-quality product:

Read the Ingredient List: Look for pesto brands with minimal, natural ingredients. Avoid those with excessive additives or preservatives.

Check the Expiry Date: Ensure the pesto has a reasonable shelf life and is within its freshness date.

Consider Artisanal Brands: Artisanal or small-batch pesto brands often prioritize quality and flavor.

Seek Recommendations: Ask for recommendations from friends, family, or online communities to discover reputable pesto brands.

Taste Test: Don't hesitate to try different brands to find the one that aligns with your flavor preferences.

In the end, the decision between homemade and store-bought pesto depends on your priorities. For the freshest and most customizable experience, homemade pesto is unbeatable. However, store-bought options offer convenience and are a valuable pantry staple when time is limited.

Chapter 20: Pesto Perfection: Tips, Tricks, and Troubleshooting

Mastering the Art of Pesto-Making

Pesto may seem simple, but achieving the perfect balance of flavors and textures requires attention to detail. In this chapter, we'll guide you through the art of pesto-making, sharing expert tips, tricks, and techniques to help you create pesto sauces that sing with flavor and vibrancy.

The Art of Pesto-Making

Mastering pesto-making is about achieving harmony among its key components: herbs, nuts, cheese, garlic, olive oil, and seasoning. Here's how to perfect the art:

Troubleshooting Common Pesto Problems

Even the most experienced cooks encounter challenges when making pesto. Here are common issues and how to troubleshoot them:

1. Bitter Pesto:

Cause: Overloading on bitter herbs like arugula or using too much garlic.

Solution: Balance the bitterness with additional basil or a milder herb. Reduce the amount of garlic, or blanch it before adding it to the pesto.

2. Watery Pesto:

Cause: Using herbs with high water content, like spinach, or overusing oil.

Solution: Pat dry the herbs or use a salad spinner to remove excess moisture. Gradually add olive oil until you reach the desired consistency.

3. Too Thick or Dry Pesto:

Cause: Not adding enough olive oil or using aged cheese that doesn't melt well.

Solution: Gradually incorporate more olive oil until the pesto reaches the desired consistency. Use fresh, quality cheese that melts easily.

4. Pesto Turning Brown:

Cause: Exposure to air causes oxidation, leading to a brownish hue.

Solution: To prevent browning, add a squeeze of lemon juice, blanch the herbs briefly, or store the pesto in an airtight container with a thin layer of olive oil on top.

5. Pesto Separation:

Cause: Overmixing or adding hot ingredients to the pesto.

Solution: Mix pesto gently to avoid overprocessing. Allow hot ingredients to cool slightly before incorporating them.

6. Lack of Flavor:

Cause: Not using enough salt or missing the balance of ingredients.

Solution: Taste and adjust. Add more salt or any missing elements like garlic, nuts, or cheese to achieve a balanced flavor.

Expert Tips and Tricks for Pesto Perfection

Here are some expert tips and tricks to elevate your pesto-making game:

1. Use a Food Processor:

A food processor ensures even blending and a smoother texture. If you don't have one, a blender can work, but it may require more scraping and patience.

2. Toast Nuts:

Toasting nuts enhances their flavor. Toast them in a dry skillet or oven until fragrant before adding them to the pesto.

3. Adjust Ingredients Gradually:

When following a recipe, add ingredients like olive oil, garlic, and salt gradually, tasting as you go to reach the desired balance.

4. Fresh Ingredients Are Key:

Use the freshest herbs, nuts, and cheese you can find for the best flavor. Consider growing your own herbs for ultimate freshness.

5. Store Pesto Properly:

If making in advance, store pesto in an airtight container with a layer of olive oil on top to prevent browning and oxidation.

6. Get Creative:

Pesto is versatile. Experiment with different herbs, nuts, and cheeses to create your unique pesto variations.

7. Pair Thoughtfully:

Consider the dishes you'll serve with your pesto and tailor the sauce to complement their flavors.

Mastering the art of pesto-making requires practice and a willingness to adjust and refine your technique. With these tips, tricks, and troubleshooting strategies, you're well on your way to pesto perfection.

In this cookbook, we've taken you on a journey through the world of pesto, from classic Genovese to international variations, vegan and seasonal pesto, and even pesto-themed parties. Armed with these skills and insights, your pesto creations are sure to impress and delight.

Congratulations! You've embarked on a culinary journey through the vibrant and delicious world of pesto. From classic Genovese to international variations, vegan and seasonal pesto, and even pesto-themed parties, you've explored the versatility of this beloved sauce. Along the way, you've gained valuable insights, expert tips, and troubleshooting skills to create pesto sauces that are nothing short of perfection.

Pesto is more than just a sauce; it's a celebration of fresh ingredients, creativity, and the joy of sharing flavorful meals with loved ones. Whether you choose to craft your pesto from scratch or opt for quality store-bought options, your pesto creations are sure to elevate your culinary repertoire.

As you continue your culinary adventures, remember that pesto is a canvas waiting for your artistic touch. Don't be afraid to experiment with herbs, nuts, cheeses, and other ingredients to create your unique pesto masterpieces.

Thank you for joining us on this flavorful journey through the world of pesto. We hope this cookbook has inspired your creativity in the kitchen and added a dash of pesto magic to your meals. Whether you're a seasoned chef or a novice cook, pesto is a delightful companion on your culinary voyage.

Keep exploring, experimenting, and savoring the rich, vibrant flavors of homemade pesto. Your culinary adventure has just begun, and there are countless more pesto creations waiting to be discovered. Happy cooking, and may your pesto always be a source of joy and deliciousness in your life.

Bon appétit!

Milton Keynes UK
Ingram Content Group UK Ltd.
UKHW012247291123
433483UK00001B/72

9 798215 386149